Jane and t
How much in ...
have you on life's ...
Jim

WHAT DO YOU
SAY?

Learning to Listen for Grace
Among Our Elders

SECOND EDITION

JAMES A. CAMPBELL

SUNBURY
P R E S S
Mechanicsburg, PA USA

Published by Sunbury Press, Inc.
105 South Market Street
Mechanicsburg, Pennsylvania 17055

www.sunburypress.com

For information about special discounts for bulk purchases, please contact Sunbury Press Orders Dept. at (855) 338-8359 or orders@sunburypress.com.

To request one of our authors for speaking engagements or book signings, please contact Sunbury Press Publicity Dept. at publicity@sunburypress.com.

ISBN: 978-1-62006-697-3 (Trade Paperback)
ISBN: 978-1-62006-698-0 (Mobipocket)

Library of Congress Control Number: 2016935551

FIRST SUNBURY PRESS EDITION: April 2016

Product of the United States of America
0 1 1 2 3 5 8 13 21 34 55

Set in Bookman Old Style
Designed by Crystal Devine
Cover by Amber Rendon
Edited by Jennifer Cappello
All photography courtesy of Doris Bingham

Continue the Enlightenment!

Dedicated To
Richard Randall
for his support
through the ministry of this story,
for his friendship
through lone valleys and high mountains,
and for his blessing
when written works were birthed
from life to parable.

We are the sum of our stories.

CONTENTS

PREFACE

As a child, I would visit my grandmother, Eloise Campbell, on her Illinois farm in the summers. Those weeks were magical times. We'd eat ice cream constantly, play round after round of mini-golf, go to movies and church, and sit on the porch watching the sunset over the cornfields. The sky would light up with the deepest reds and oranges I had ever seen.

Every day, Grandma would walk around her cozy brick house and talk to me about each of her knickknacks. There were quite a few. There was the crystal bowl given by a cousin; the macadamia wood coasters a friend brought her from Hawaii; the china she had inherited from her mother. It was amazing she could remember it all.

I admit I was not particularly interested most of the time. I did not know any of the people she was talking about. But I tried to ask questions because these things seemed important to her. Only later did I realize that talking about these objects—and the people and stories behind them—was her way of connecting me to her world.

My experiences with my grandmother helped inspire me to become a geriatrician. Today, I have the privilege of caring for older adults in my office, a nursing home, and on visits to my patients' homes. And I have found that the key to being a good geriatrician is to listen.

"Listen to your patient," Sir William Osler, cofounder of Johns Hopkins Hospital, once said. "He is telling you the diagnosis."

My years in medicine have borne this out. When I have diagnosed something that has been missed by others, it is often because I took the time to listen to the patient's full story. I tell the medical residents and geriatric fellows I teach that being a good geriatrician means knowing your patients' medical complaints as well as you know your medicine.

It also means listening for clues to their social situation. I need to know what is going on in my patients' lives to know how to help them. How do they spend their days? Who gets their groceries or does their laundry? Are they struggling with loneliness? I love to see family pictures and hear stories of grandchildren. Those photos and stories tell me that my patients may have people in their lives to help them when they need it.

The value of listening that I have learned in my medical practice is something that my second cousin, Jim Campbell, knows well from his own work as a pastor. It is something he experienced especially through his ministry to the residents of Iowa's Dunlap Care Center. In this eloquent book, Jim shares the lessons he learned from those men and women, and from a lifetime of sharing the Gospel with others by truly listening to what they had to say.

One of those to whom Jim listened was my grandmother. While Jim was earning his master's degree at the University of Illinois in the 1970s, he would visit Eloise, ask her about the history of our family, and listen to her stories. They wound up creating a genealogy that fascinated me when I later discovered it as a teenager.

Eloise died in 2006. Shortly before her final decline, when I was in my late twenties, I bought a tape recorder to try to capture some of her tales. But by then her health and memory were failing. She had moved to a nursing home and was no longer surrounded by the objects that helped her remember. What I would have given to be back in that little farmhouse, walking around all those bowls and coasters and listening to those wonderful stories.

I encourage you to soak up the deep wisdom of this book, wisdom born of Jim's years of ministry to elders. Take these words to heart while those you love can still tell you their stories, and you can still listen.

John A. Campbell, MD
Physician of Geriatric Medicine

INTRODUCTION

It is autumn as I write these lines; my favorite time of the year. The heat of the summer has given way to the more tempered days and nights of fall. The burst of summer growth has ripened into the quiet maturity of harvest time. One must have eyes to see the beauty and bounty of these autumn days. The falling leaves, the shriveled vines, and the drooping ears of every cornfield can be deceiving. Without wisdom and an experienced eye, this bounty could be overlooked.

James Campbell tells us about the rich harvest that lies close to all of us who are caregivers as family members or as professionals. He does so with the wisdom, grace, and skill of an artist, gradually revealing the beauty hidden by stereotype, ignorance, and tradition.

He tells us about becoming a strong listener, dancing the lame duck, whooping, discovering sacred space, and most of all, he pulls back the curtain on the mystery of life itself. Every life. And as the curtain parts we see the stories of courage, faith, and hope of those in the autumn years of life. If we look carefully, we may even see ourselves and hear echoes of our own life story.

This book does not offer six simple steps to effective ministry with aging persons. It does offer a way of listening and seeing that can open all of us to the rich harvest of life within and around us. I commend to you the practice of learning to listen for grace.

Rueben P. Job
October 1990

Review by the Publisher
from the First Edition

"What do you say? Really, what do you say? You open your Bible at the makeshift pulpit before twenty or thirty sets of eyes. You are not sure if some even comprehend where they are, let alone who you are. Some eyes are dull, tranquilized eyes, while others dart here and there like tiny birds."

Thus does James A. Campbell lead the way into the realm of pastoral ministry in care settings for older adults. What do you say in such settings? Campbell is unflinchingly honest about the question. More than anything, he wants to know where and how grace is found in such ministry settings; and his answer is simple, direct, touching, and passionate: "You don't say. You listen." Finely wrought accounts of shared humor, pathos, history, and heritage show why listening to and with older adults is one of the surest ways to connect with the grace that sustains us all. This is a book for every person who wants to remember and practice the deep sources of ministry in care settings for older adults.

EMPATHETIC KNOWING

It may be that the future belongs to those of multiple ways of knowing. One way of knowing is learning to listen well, and in the witness of this work, to listen well to our elders.

Empathetic knowing is more than an inherited gift of time and caring; it is an awareness of the depth and beauty of others, cultivated with much intentionality. Empathy is learned. Listening well is learned.

The lives discovered in this volume hopefully inspire the reader to see the blessing waiting to be given by the aged. Even more, it is hoped that empathy toward some becomes an inspiration of empathy to a hurting, frenzied, fearful world.

What greater gift could our elders avail than to help us discover a grammar of listening, a discipline of empathetic knowing, an enlightenment to a more humane, engaged and accepting openness to all people?

J.A.C.

PART 1:
THE STORY

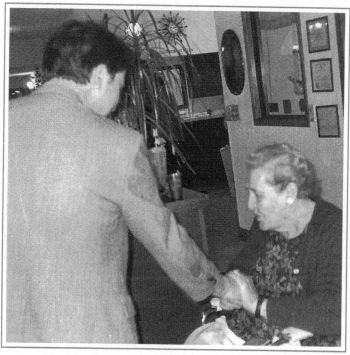

The blessing of one hand, one story, to another.

WHAT DO YOU SAY?

What do you say?
Really,
What do you say?
You open your Bible at the makeshift
pulpit before twenty or thirty sets of eyes.
You are not sure if some even comprehend
where they are, let alone who you are. Some
eyes are dull, tranquilized eyes, while others
dart here and there like nervous tiny birds.
Still others placidly wait in acceptance. You
wonder how long they have been waiting in
those chairs. Chairs are more than furniture
here. Chairs seem to be the symbol of the
place, symbols of waiting—waiting for what?
Waiting to wait some more. No, be honest,
waiting to die. Chairs of waiting. When you
go, you leave behind an empty chair . . . for a
day, before someone else falls in line to wait.

"Lord, what a dismal place." As you say
that under your breath, you ask yourself
again, "What do you say?" How do you enter
this world of empty existence, a world of
bingo for bananas, hourly strolls to the lobby,
and the endlessly blaring television? Is it any
wonder that many older people fight nursing
homes as though they were worse than
death? "Shoot me. Put me out of my misery,
but don't put me in one of those hell holes."

They mean it. They dread nursing homes more than death. Nursing homes are no way to conclude one's life. Living isn't living when all the colors have been washed from existence. What is existence that is wasted gazing out of institutional windows to sprawling institutional lawns or sharing institutional food with those who have become childish and rude in their feebleness?

"Don't send me here to be forgotten and then doped up to endure nothingness in the stench of those who have lost control of their bodily functions. Don't send me here where my life savings are gone in a year or two, leaving me with no sense of worth in any manner—a spiritual, emotional, fiscal ward of the state. Don't leave me."

Such are the words that fill your mind as you study the eyes that face you: the eyes of those who gave in, resigned to the fact that life must go on even if it has no reason. Again the echo captures your attention. "What do you say?" What can you say to give meaning and hope to such existence? What is the good news of God's love to those who live in a drab, lifeless box where nothing matters but the 2:00 pill?

What do you say?

I remember preaching in a care facility where one fellow who had to be restrained kept interrupting my sermon by yelling, "Prove it! Prove it!" It was most disconcerting, especially since the sermon was so milquetoast that there was nothing to prove. Only later did I realize that in challenging my emptiness he was crying out against his own.

What do you say?

Indeed, what do you say? After all, these people are being comforted. Everywhere you hear soft voices consoling, reminding, affirming. Kindness in some care facilities may be a façade, but most genuinely strive to make kindness the standard. Yet how could a standard of kindness be warped into punishment? "Shoot me before you send me there—anywhere, anything but that."

As you greet the people after the worship, a woman in a wheelchair takes your hand. No, she grabs your hand. She says something about her daughter. Her words ebb and rise in volume like the music from a distant radio station. Her disconnected chatter becomes her continued excuse to maintain her hold. You listen for a couple minutes. Politely, firmly, you reach with your other hand and release her grasp as you take charge of the conversation and set her free. No, you set yourself free.

Beside this woman sits another, a total contrast. Her hair is well groomed. Her printed silk dress bears a large brooch of a style long forgotten. She sits erect, thoughtful. She thanks you for coming and waits patiently for the less mobile to be helped to their rooms.

What must this place mean to her? What must it mean to be constantly reminded of the indignity of what is ahead? Behind her on the wall is a sign that reads, "Today is Wednesday," as if she needed to be reminded. Around her are voices of visitors speaking to residents as though addressing children. Perhaps she has accepted it. You wonder, and in the wonder you wonder all the more, what do you say?

Then again, perhaps you're too concerned. Maybe these people can't see through the song and dance you're doing. But maybe they can. A friend who lives at a care facility sees the pastors come and go and writes: "I've seen this scene so often. Most pastors come with their own agenda. I doubt if any of them really *think* to whom they are speaking. It's just another, less responsive, congregation."

Yes, some do see, and as they see the shallowness of your words, what must they think of the worship and themselves?

The scene changes to a tiny, nondescript bungalow with slightly tilted venetian blinds partly pulled, partly hiding its occupant in the extended shadows of ill-kept trees and bushes. This is the home of Lila. Lila is eighty-two years old. She lives alone and bears the label "semi-shut-in." She gets out, but only with considerable effort and with some help. She still takes care of her home, though not with the thoroughness of earlier years. Like Lila herself, her surroundings are fading—fading pictures, fading wallpaper, fading rugs and furniture, sun-bleached drapes. Beside her overstuffed sofa is a china cabinet crowded with knickknacks that seem to have spilled out into the room, occupying every available inch of shelf space that isn't already taken by a violet.

You sit across from Lila, leaning forward with hands together in that "let's make conversation" pose. What follows is a polite walk through the garden of old age topics. Aches and pains, the weather, the prices these days, who is in the hospital, comments about a niece you have never met who just got a job in Albuquerque, and her fears of neighborhood vandals.

Total elapsed time: five minutes. She inquires about your family and your work. Total elapsed time: three minutes.

Eight minutes. That's it. You look out the window for some focus for further conversation. After all, you should stay for at least fifteen minutes. But what do you say? Do you talk about knickknacks and violets? Do you probe the depths of her soul? Do you ask the obvious, "Lila, are you lonely?" If she were honest enough to reply "yes," what would you say? Of course, you could cut it all short by saying an extended prayer that covers the world's problems and a good five minutes. You picture Lila in prayer on those rare Sundays when she would venture out and join her comrades in widows' row in the back of the church. How often did you wonder to yourself, what do these women pray for? What do they get out of a sermon? What does it mean to be here? What do they really want from me? What do they want from anyone, really? Family, neighbors—they too must come here and wonder after eight minutes: What do you say?

One thing is for sure—whatever you say is work, duty. As a pastor I state it bluntly: Speaking of hope is the hardest of ministries to those whose life's beginnings are over.

Your burden, and the burden of all who love them, is to help them cope; to cope with waiting . . . waiting to die.

As you see that task, the question looms all the greater. What do you say to people with such time on their hands?

Before you, the reader, answer in quick response and with the certainty of your insights of old age and your theological convictions, I ask you to think again. Are you sure it's the right question?

RIBBONS AND WAVES

Before Mary died, she gathered around her hospital bed those persons most significant to her life. One by one she shared why each person was important to her, how each one had influenced her living. As she spoke, she untied and gave to each person a piece of ribbon that had been knotted to the next. Together, all the pieces of the ribbon had created a whole—just as each of her friendships had woven together to aid the wholeness of her own living. The ribbon was a memento of life's meaning found in connectedness, life woven into life.

I liked Mary's gesture, though at the time I didn't realize the depth of all she was suggesting. There is an obvious truth to Mary's ribbon. Our lives do intertwine. There is more, however, to the connectedness than people weaving together shared experiences. Genuine friendship absorbs character. Character is the essence and force of a person's story. As we come to trust, so do we yield more and more of our story and our character and its energy. Likewise, we absorb the memories and power of those who grace us with their tales, good and bad, odd and common. As we imagine their pasts, the character and force of our friends' stories become part of us, inspiring and moving us. What they have experienced that still moves them, is moving us.

We may never have directly experienced the Great Depression, what it was like to live without electricity, the emergence of the first automobile; but through the stories of those who have experienced these events, we too have touched and have been touched by those very moments. Through our friends' telling, we can yet feel the force of those moments like ripples from a rock dropped into a lake. The energy of the ripple continues to lap the shore though the rock has disappeared.

Much like the ripple of a lake, I understand that when I turn on the television to a channel that has no signal, the chaotic, static

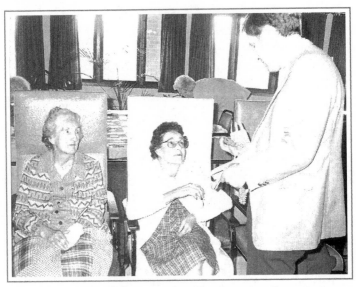

And what was that like for you ...?

interference I receive is actually the continuing echo, the rippling of the big bang of creation's first moment. If rippling in nature can be true, if I can touch the ripple of the very beginning of time, how much more is it true that I can receive in a friend's confidence the rippling influence of events far before and far away from my own time and place. It is altogether possible for one who is only 30 years old to have lived moments three quarters of a century before his/her birth and half a world away from his/her most distant journey . . . if . . . if that person is willing to really absorb the gifts of story that are given.

We treat conversation so casually, so benignly, as something so incidental to life. It's all so much chat. Yet in the perceived dull ore of chat, there are sacred metals. Few people are more empowered with life than those who can genuinely listen and lose themselves in another person's story. Such listening becomes an empowerment to the storyteller who, in being taken seriously, is allowed to feel in his or her own telling just how much life really means and how much energy past experiences still have to give.

We lie on the crest of a wave. The energy of the momentum of past generations is below us, carrying us on, even as we become a part of the wave for those who follow. Most people live their lives on the crest with little thought to the quiet energy that is carrying them. That is their choice, *but it is a choice.*

We can also choose in tying the ribbons of acquaintances to seek out the energies of life that reach back in time, reach down into the wave that carries us in every sense of story—artistically, historically, biographically, and, in it all, spiritually. We have a choice in how we listen. In that choice we decide the depth of our living.

Once I had a funeral for a woman who was 102 years old. In preparation for the funeral, I found from her children that she, as a little girl, had come with her family to Iowa in a covered wagon. How I wish that I had talked with her for just a little while. I could have. I just didn't. How I long to have listened, to have sensed even the faintest ripple of waves from a time when the last of the pioneers were arriving to this yet untilled earth.

At the same time, an aunt of mine died. She left behind a large box of letters—450 pages of letters. They were letters of my father's family, of their hopes and struggles from 1915 to 1932. As I read, sorted, and filed them, there emerged a deep appreciation for my grandmother. No longer was she just the sweet old lady for whom I held skeins to roll into yarn balls that turned into afghans. She was no longer just Grandma in all the wonderful ways she was Grandma at birthdays and Christmases. No, suddenly, she was a young woman with three children, huddled for the night with my grandfather under an overturned horse wagon on the virgin prairies of North Dakota, dreaming of what the open prairie could be. Letters later, she was a widow alone on that same isolated prairie in the middle of the Depression. Alone she took her children across the plains a thousand miles in an open-top Model T Ford.

I could not put the letters down. I was drawn more and more into the spirit of this woman—blood of my blood—whose life was gone but for these letters, the memories of her surviving children, and the echo of her voice. She had died only seven years earlier. No one had bothered to record her voice, let alone her story. It would have taken only an afternoon.

Between the funeral for this aged parishioner and the letters of my grandmother, something clicked. Suddenly I wanted to touch as much of the living past as I could. I wanted to listen, selfishly listen. I wanted to step through the cold pages of my history books like Alice through her looking glass. I wanted to reach through as far as I could to those who would tell me of life. I wanted to hear of days far beyond my reach, still rippling with life—life that was mine to have for the listening; life to give meaning, energy, and focus to my own calling as a storyteller.

I felt compelled to become for a while a story listener. I decided I would go to a nursing home seeking those souls who would

17

tie their ribbons to mine and help me feel and absorb the wave of creation from which I was born and upon which I live my routines. It was as if I were seeking some additional blessing to my ordination. I would not go with pity in my eyes and speak condescendingly about the weather. No, I would go passionately to listen. I would go to the nursing home seeking to be *ministered* to by these frail people who seemingly had nothing in life to live for.

What do you say to people in care facilities, to shut-ins, to any person who by consensus has reached that point of being old?

Nothing.

If you really care about them, you go to listen.

You go to be blessed.

WHOOP

Not everyone finds energy from the past, however well put the need for it. Those who don't have a heart for history must find their own route to serving those whose lives are mostly history. You can't be what you aren't. Ministry is an art and it must be shared as an art. It is not, in the end, a matter of technique learned and principles applied, with the certainty of a paint-by-number outcome. Growth comes in finding those spirits who compel us to say "yes," who bring out our own interests and talents to create, or who make us angry enough to rebel, who are irritatingly vague in vision so as to compel us to focus our truth.

Given the above, I hope the reader will not passively press on, viewing this as a how-to-do-it manual. Rather, if we be of kindred spirits, then continue while listening to your own hunches the impulse that says, "If it were me I would have . . ." Then care enough to act on your own impulses. The world is full of older people living and dying with wasted blessings.

All of this serves as a preface to whooping. The word *whoop* came to me in the midst of working with older people. It came into my life like a stray dog. "Whoop" just rolled off my tongue one day. At first I was guarded in its use and embarrassed when caught being lost in the ecstasy of its expression. Then I learned I was not alone. There were other whoopers. A college in Texas whoops instead of cheering at football games. Years ago, the mayor of Portland, Oregon, whooped. Few things in life are more exhilarating than a good, uninhibited whoop—especially down the hall of a senior citizens' care facility. To be sure, such expression needs the blessing of the care facility's staff. It also takes a while for the residents to adjust. The initial blast of a good whoop has been known to cause a noticeable rise of an occupant from a wheelchair. Those who have been dozing may suddenly awake, asking apologetically, "Was that me?"

Eventually, the Thursday morning whoop at the Dunlap Care Center became routine, something like the testing of a disaster siren. At times I would forget to whoop. Residents who had gathered for our sessions would become concerned.

"Aren't you feeling well?"

"What's the problem?"

I would then have to exit the room, go halfway down the hall, and give a good whoop in order to start the session on a proper note.

In time, whooping led to the shedding of any ecclesiastical or academic pretense. The pastor became addressed as the "whoop-whoop" man or "Slick," which is another story.

There is good reason to question the why of whooping. In part, the whoop was used to deliberately upset preconceptions—not just those folks' ideas about a pastor, but mine about nursing home residents. Whooping disarms. It creates a delightful atmosphere of momentary disorientation. It also sets the tone of our togetherness. In a sense, our zany community's trust, laughter, and revelations boiled down to whooping. It was in the spirit of the whoop that I one day received from them a mug. These 85- to 95-year-olds had painted a mug that had been formed in the shape of the hindquarters of a horse. The mug read, "There's one in every church."

Again, this is one person's ministry. It is not offered as advice. Not every member of the clergy, not every care center administrator, not every nurse, not every son or daughter of an older person would appreciate the finesse of whooping. Nor would everyone who appreciates the spirit of whoop be inclined to imitate.

So be it.

Such is art.

Such is ministry.

THE LAME DUCK

Dunlap Care Center stands watch over the small Iowa town that gives it its name. At the bottom of the hill to the north is a small fishing pond. To the west and south is a panorama of the rolling farmland and timber stands of the Boyer Valley. The view is worthy of a cross-stitch pattern. It is that and more. The care center perches above the stage where most of its residents played out the fullness of their lives. To understand the setting is to know its people. To know its people is to wonder all the more at the parables of life the seasons of this view provide.

Each Thursday I came up here, exchanged yarns with the administrator, and whooped my way to the craft room to greet a dozen to 20 people who had gathered around their unfinished ceramic projects. Some were in chairs; others, wheelchairs. Some were blind; others, partially paralyzed. Some were anxious to share; others quietly fell asleep. So be it. Whatever the mood of the day or the condition of the resident, I was there to claim a blessing.

The session began with each person sharing his or her past week:, letters received, physical concerns, a passing anecdote. We noted who wasn't there due to illness. We traded jokes. I shared the struggles of newly attained fatherhood. From such concerns emerged our prayers; from our prayers came the devotions that they, the residents, brought—devotions they had found in a week of their own spiritual journeys.

From these devotions the doors of the past opened. Sometimes it took a question. "Tell me of life around your mother's kitchen stove. Tell me of the smells of the fields, the cream separator room, the granary. Tell me about horse rides and Saturday nights. Tell me of storms and floods and snowdrifts. Tell me about the first cars and airplanes, the first radio you ever heard, the Sears Roebuck catalog, reading by a kerosene lamp. Tell me of the sounds of the harvest, the corn hitting the buckboard, the threshing machine, the conversations of the threshing crew. Tell me of the view from your schoolhouse window. Tell me of your very favorite hiding place."

Sometimes it took an object, perhaps a cornhusking peg. They would show me how to use it, and from its use emerged stories of the good years, or the extreme drought where a whole harvest was gathered in less than one wagonload. How I remember one woman who, from when I first met her, had never said a word. I was not sure of her affliction, and, until I handed her the cornhusking peg, I wasn't sure she was even cogent of the meeting. As she took the peg, her eyes bore such wonder and satisfaction. She never spoke of what she saw and felt as she molded it over and over in her hand. I just knew she understood. I knew that I had touched the meaning of the distant past however faintly it rippled into the present.

In conversations about the past emerged fascinating words and the living that gave them meaning. One phrase was "water glass," which was not a glass at all, but a powder that, when added to water, preserved eggs in the cold months when the hens weren't laying. "Asafetida" was a hideous smelling ball of "medicine" that dangled from a string necklace to ward off colds and, I would think, anything or anyone else. Then there was the Lame Duck.

The Lame Duck was not an afflicted bird or an impotent politician. No, it was a pre-World War II dance with rather afflicted, contorted moves that mimicked a wounded duck. Such suggests but certainly doesn't fully describe this zany, off-the-wall dance. No doubt its humor provided a much needed escape from the dreary grips of the Depression.

Now imagine a pastor who has no natural dance rhythm or grace negotiating the Lame Duck with a woman in a wheelchair in a space of four square feet. The rest of the group is stomping and clapping as best it can. The resulting commotion prompted an ecstasy of laughter that compelled the care center staff to finally check in on the matter. The staff's amazed silence is yet one of my favorite memories of ministry.

HALF OF HUMAN HISTORY

The more I probed and absorbed the blessing of the world of my care center friends, the more I realized just how far into the depths of history I was able to reach. Assume that author Alvin Toffler is right. Assume that more change has happened in the past century than in all the prior centuries of history combined. If that is true, even partially true, imagine the energy of the past that is ours to claim by simply absorbing the lives of those who have lived the fullness of the past century.

In our conversations, I felt the fear of gypsies who once traveled the back roads and terrorized the imaginations of farm folk. I knew of intense loyalty to neighbors who helped deliver each other's babies, harvested each other's crops, and provided each other entertainment on front porches that were essential to daily life. I also felt the dark side of those same clannish relationships, an intimacy that fostered deep suspicion and hatred toward those who were different.

Occasionally, something would come from the group quite matter-of-factly, something so taken for granted that its mention needed no explanation except to me.

For example, there was March 1st. March 1st had never been of special interest to me until it emerged in casual conversation in the group. March 1st was moving day. Farmers always moved on March 1st. This day was especially important to those farmers who rented and changed farms every year. They would pack up everything, including the heating stoves, and move down the lane with their herds of livestock in front of them.

From this discussion, I learned that though persons might move several times in their lives, the next place almost always was within a few miles of the place before. Any number of the group had never gone more than 25 miles in any direction by the time they were 20 years old. To really listen was to keep these stirred-up gifts from resettling, unnoticed, back on the ocean floor.

I was amazed at such isolation and the excitement of March 1st. I was equally amazed that these people who once frequented the hotel and train station on Saturday night just to feel the wonder of a world beyond their horizon, would live to travel thousands of miles by airplane to visit children and grandchildren as satellites orbited the earth. Half the history of change of the human race was recorded in their faces.

In another session, someone mentioned the "Farmers' Holiday." It was neither a day on the calendar nor a celebration. It was a time of protest during the Depression by those farmers who had had enough and went on strike against the system. Many went to jail. Other farmers refused on moral grounds to dispose of much of their livestock, which the government demanded, in order to drive up prices.

I had never heard of the Farmers' Holiday until this group told me about it. Nor had I ever really considered how much meaning, how much clarity of thought and values emerged from the hurt of those Depression days. They were the worst of times; yet, understandably, in retrospect, they were for my group the most meaningful years of their lives. To touch, through them, that time's peculiar joys, simple beauties, and intense hope in community gave my own life hope and determination during a spell of personal anguish. Through my own depression I came back again and again to the blessing, the empowerment of those who had endured the Depression. For some time I dwelled with the group on their stories of the Depression, not just because they wanted to tell and I wanted to listen, but because I needed their healing. In the midst of one of those sessions on finding meaning in struggle, I asked the group to go as far back in their lives as memory would allow to a time when they were afraid. Could they remember being afraid as a child?

"Yes, I can remember," said Winnie. Winnie was in her late eighties, which made her five or six years old when her story took place. "Mom had died. Dad had all of us kids and couldn't cope. He needed a wife, and that's what he set out to find. He put all of us kids in the custody of an orphanage with the promise to return as soon as he could.

"I was put on a floor with other girls my age in the keeping of a matron whose discipline was as dreadful as it was effective. If you did anything wrong, she would dunk your head in a bucket of water until you fought desperately for air. I hated her. The place was a nightmare.

"Well, Dad did come back, and we children became a family once again with our new mother. One day Dad took us to the fair, and amidst the crowd I spotted her, the witch [from the orphanage]. I became so upset, so angry, I began screaming, pointing at her, telling my father of her terrible acts.

"My sudden commotion drew the attention of everyone, including a politician giving an open air speech. Making the most of the interruption, he had me brought to him. He tried to appease me before the crowd by offering me a little white bear. I didn't want his little white bear. I told him I wanted a ride on the merry-go-round. I should have settled for the bear. The politician was Teddy Roosevelt."

I sat amazed. Amazed at the richness of experience with which she had answered that question and others; amazed how I was blessed to touch such a magnificent distant moment of history through the eyes of a little girl. I was in awe of my little group. Here were those I had once perceived as glassy-eyed stares waiting for the next pill. Here were those waiting to die with nothing to offer but a job for someone to take care of them. I was wrong. We all are wrong. It is we who have glassy eyes. What wastes away in nursing homes, in the homes of shut-ins, and on the widows' row of our churches is our own blessing—the energy, meaning, and healing of half of human history slipping through our fingers.

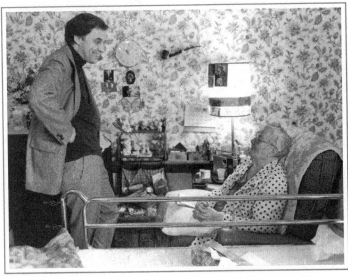

Reverend James Campbell with Winnie Bonsall

SHARING THE BLESSING

I called the local newspaper editor. I had a story for her, and then another. There was Winnie and her encounter with Roosevelt and her peace pipe on the wall, which was given to her father by an Indian chief. There was Henry, who had repaired the very first airplanes used in combat during World War I. Lois was an independent-minded, range-riding cowgirl in the '30s. There was Fred, whose weathered farmer's hands chronicled the past century in a sculpture of callouses.

With permission, these experiences found their way into several media—into news articles, sermons, and one evening, into a youth group discussion. With a tape recorder running, I asked my senior high youth to think of what it would be like to live in a care facility, to be a shut-in, or to just be old. I asked, "What do you think it was like to be young seventy years ago?" The probing and reflecting went on for more than an hour. It was a delightful evening. It was even more delightful to see the interest and hear the laughter of my old folks as they commented on what they heard on the tape. They in turn discussed before my tape recorder what they perceived as the experience of growing up today. Back and forth the taping went, amusing, enlightening, and sensitizing both groups to each other.

The bottom line of these discussions was this: "We in the nursing home are not suffering; we are not to be pitied. We are very much alive, thank you, and well taken care of. Life is good now, and though times have changed, we know the feeling of being young, in love, and frustrated with parents. It also feels good to be taken seriously."

In the discussion some sensitive issues came out. One young person asked, "What do you miss?" The answer was candid. With spouses gone and children far away, older adults have a real longing to be touched, to be hugged. That is one reason the presence of small children has such importance for older people. It gives one a reason to hug and be hugged.

They missed other things. "A steak dinner, I mean a big juicy steak!" Another said, "Do you know how many years it's been since I've had spring mushrooms, morel mushrooms?"

That spring, with the help of a fellow connoisseur of mushrooms in a neighboring town, a large mess of morel mushrooms was gathered and prepared by the care center staff. A few weeks later, the church provided the funds for a special dinner. Those who wanted it and whose diet would permit it had top-of-the-line steak.

As this ministry unfolded, it caught the attention of the Iowa Health Care Association.

At the association's annual convention in 1983, the Dunlap Care Center ministry had its moment. It was a moment of appreciation for the lives and liveliness of the Dunlap Care Center's residents.

Winnie, Fred, and Henry are no longer living—except in the momentum of the energy of their shared lives that extended to those who cared to listen and now to tell what they heard.

How terrible to think of someday being old with a story to tell and a blessing to give, yet no one is interested. For all the concern about ecology, about preserving our resources, no resource is more carelessly wasted than the blessing of the old, withering in a silence of thoughtless relatives who visit and talk of the weather, or clergy who come to preach with nothing to say yet preach anyway.

PART II:
THE LESSONS

We need those who teach us how to age.

NEED IS NOT A
ONE-WAY STREET

Why is there even an issue? Why doesn't one generation naturally, instinctively claim the blessings of the generations that precede it? I would ask of the nursing home residents, "What does your family think of what you have done with your life?" The reply: "They aren't interested."

But why?

Well, some people just aren't interested in the past. The present matters. History, collecting antiques, and stories of the good ol' days just don't give life purpose. There is, for some, a philosophical justification for this. The rapid changes of life are supposedly so radical that even the immediate past has no relevance to the "electric now."

Others aren't interested because life is fast-paced. Like it or not, listening to Grandma in "that creepy place"—in her home or in the nursing home—drives them up the wall. Besides, they have heard Grandma's stories at *least* once every Thanksgiving, Christmas, and family reunion.

True, they heard the stories, and they politely listened a second and third time, but they didn't lose themselves in the stories. There is a difference. Still, we get the point.

Other reasons are given. The past is not something to celebrate. Its hurts are sleeping dogs that have been aroused too many times and won't go away. Just leave the past alone. Others marry into families whose traditions, stories, and storytellers are more dominant and possessive than their family of origin. Others have moved far away, and the occasional visit has become an ever-awkward greeting of strangers.

Whatever the merit of these reasons, there is one that by its subtle, chronic, and widespread nature deserves our special attention: Grandma and Grandpa have brought much of their isolation upon themselves. This will be our plight also unless we challenge one of our most sacred virtues.

From birth until we stand on our own, we receive two messages. First, "Mom and Dad love you and are here to take care of you. We are here to bless you." The greatest accolade we pay our parents is to say, "They were always there when we needed them."

The second message follows closely on the heels of the first: "You'll never have to worry about us or take care of us. We have made provisions for our old age. We are sufficient now and will be then. You go out and make your own lives. Your happiness is all we ask."

That message rings with such truth, such compassion! That's the way it should be.

Look closely, however, for implied in this truth is another truth: *Need is a one-way street. You need us.* It seems terribly wrong, selfish, and manipulative for parents to say to their children, "We need you." But this is not true. Quite the contrary. It is a healthy relationship where the parent can say honestly, "I need to see myself living on in you. I need to know in time that I can be vulnerable and open with you, as you have been with me. I need you to know that I am stronger in adversity when you are aware and care about my struggling. I need you to know that no joy is truly complete until I have shared it with you. I need to talk with you even when I have nothing to say. I need you to know that even as I bless you and set you free to go and do what you will, *I also need your blessing.* No, even though I take care of myself, I am not totally sufficient. I need you; even if by telephone, I need you."

Some children seem naturally aware of their parents' need for them. They give intuitively of their own spirit even as they eagerly absorb through their parents the energies of the past.

Others, however, many others, go through life taking their parents' self-sufficiency at face value. Many have no sense that their parents, who love them deeply, need them in return. They have picked up the message well: "We'll take care of you. Don't worry about us." For children with parents whose independent spirit allows for little expression of feeling, accepting those ideas is especially easy. How often have you heard, "You know your father really cares; he just can't express it." Everyone also knows that your father holds the doors for others, picks up the check, and says in a hundred other ways, "I care and will give the shirt off my back but need nothing in return." In fact, he is awkward at receiving gifts and affection, even as he secretly yearns for it.

Joe was dying of a sudden and vicious disease. In the panic of it all, life's pretense fell, and this very human, frightened, vulnerable man cried out for his children. When they came, they were taken aback and embarrassed by their father's emotion. This man who through the years had said in every way, "I'm self-sufficient," was suddenly, desperately in need—honestly, nakedly in need of being held. One child, seeing the father's outstretched hand, refused to take it and left the room. Dad, after all, *had violated his own truth.* That same violation comes to others in old age when, in hunger for their children, they cry out only to hear the echo of their own words fulfilled: "Don't worry about us."

In fact, children can learn in positive, *un-crippling ways*—even from an early age—that they are not only loved but *needed.* Children often find their greatest blessing when, in growing up, there comes a moment when they realize they have the power to give love and meaning to their parents' vulnerabilities. The growing-up years are also a time when parents can learn to risk being open about their own needs without becoming manipulative and possessive. Such a foundation can turn the *yielding* of one generation to another into the *joining* of generations, and can break the isolation and purposelessness of old age and its stories.

Ministry to older persons begins with ministry to all the generations who occupy our pews. It begins by teaching the young that they are needed and have a blessing to give.

"MOM NICHOLS"

Parenting is never over, at least not for some. A beloved woman in my hometown, a woman in her nineties, was named "Mom Nichols." It was interesting that she was "Mom" to a wide variety of friends in their fifties, sixties, and seventies. I now know why. Even as we advance in age, we have a need for a parent, a mentor, someone who can show us how to age well and even to die well. Mom Nichols was such a mentor. She hadn't lost touch with the world. She was interested and interesting.

People want to grow old this way. They want to live until they die. Few fears are as real as growing old and losing touch.

All the humor we give to senility speaks to this fear. The haunting possibilities of Alzheimer's disease and of strokes speak to this fear. Most people want to die with maturity, not infancy. It doesn't always work that way. Sometimes we grow old begging people to remember us for who we once were. It can't be helped. So be it.

Still, it is not entirely a matter of nature. It is also a matter of choice. We have some say in how we age.

My Aunt Clella died well. She too was a "mom" to those facing old age. As she made the journey from the farm to town, from her bungalow to the care center and finally to the extended care unit, she brought along her commitment to life. When she was completely bedridden, she said to me, "I can't do anything but pray for people. So that's what I do." That was her commitment to God. That was her commitment to live until she died.

Ironically, even as losing touch with life is one of the greatest fears of old age, it is also its greatest temptation. It is easy to just give in. What's more, this message is subtly promoted even by the people who love older adults most. Loved ones see in their aging family members the growing need for structure and routine. They see the irritability toward others over little things. They see the increasingly frail stature and the need for more sleep. Put it all together and it spells childlike. So, like a child, they are nursed, protected, and amused. Listen to the tone of the voice. Children have become parents to their childlike parents.

In part that is reasonable. In part we do go full circle and become the child we once were. In part we seek the security and comfort we knew as a child. In part . . . but only in part, at least only in part if we choose, for we have a choice. What's more, our adult children have a part to play in that choice.

By protecting Mom and Dad in the nursing home, we hold back the hard knocks of life. Grandma and Grandpa don't need to know that their grandchildren are struggling, that their son is unhappy with his job, and that their old neighbor has died. No, all of that would make them feel bad. Grandma comments that her son looks tired: "What's the matter?"

"Nothing. I'm all right," comes the response. Grandma knows better. She can read her son's eyes. She also can sense what his lack of response says about her.

I proceed carefully on this point that aged persons should be included more in the life of their family and not be patronized by the family or by the nursing home staff. Each person has specific needs, and many people grow older saying, "Look, I've fought the wars. I came here for peace and quiet. When you come to visit, leave your problems behind. I don't want them."

That should be respected even as others should be respected who resent exclusion from family life simply because they are old. Many of them are stronger and more insightful than we imagine.

One family held back from Grandpa that his grandson had divorced. Finally, they told him for fear he might hear it from someone else. Grandpa's response was one of sadness turned to concern for his grandson. "How is he? I want to talk with him." The conversation that followed, the encouragement and hope that Grandpa gave his grandson, not only helped the grandson get on with life but allowed the whole family to rise above its guilt and disappointment. Grandpa was still necessary. That was a needed lesson for the family and for Grandpa.

Again, this is an issue that requires discretion, mindful of each resident's needs and capabilities. It is also an issue of ministry to care center residents that needs to be faced openly. It boils down to this. If, as you grow old, you don't want to be isolated from your family's struggles, *then you need to say so.* It's part of your choice to say yes to life. It can also be the family's choice to talk about growing old as it happens, that the family moves with Grandma and Grandpa into old age instead of indirectly creating isolation and purposelessness in the guise of caring.

SACRED SPACE

I need sacred space. I need a south
window nook with sunlight playing across a
regiment of books. I need music and silence
blending with the 4:00 light and its shadows,
creating my creating.

Sometimes sacred space is defined by
more than walls and light. Sometimes sacred
space is fluid, vacillating in the give-and-take
of the parameters of friendly conversation.
Good company provides its own meaning of
sacred space.

Still another way of defining sacred space
is to note what space isn't sacred. Where is
that space least conducive to creating? Where
is that company least able to engage one's
imagination?

Years ago, with little hesitation, I would
have answered, "The homes of shut-ins and
nursing homes," which meant a holding
station of those waiting to die.

They aren't. In fact, they bear the
possibility of just the opposite. Gone are the
stereotypes of barren, off-white, institutional
walls that framed numbed faces of drugged
indifference.

Gathering with my group became for me a
sanctuary from the demands of other
ministries. The care center bore its own gift of

sacred space. In time I came to need not only the energy found in the pulse of still vital stories from the past, but the healing, the searching, the laughter, the praying of the here-and-now in a group that gave new meaning to sacred space.

Ordinarily, sacred space comes easily and naturally. We hire an architect to design a sanctuary that obeys the laws of making sacred space. Then, too, it comes in the steady flow of friendships and families around a comfortable table and a coffeepot.

Yet who is to say but what the most sacred of all spaces comes from the determination to find the sacred where it doesn't seem to first appear. It is of such hopes that pastors who loathe going to nursing homes should stand at the door in wonder and anticipation. It is there. It may take effort to realize it, become vulnerable to it, and need it. It is of such discipline of seeking the sacred in the ordinary that the real gifts of the sacred are found.

PART III:
GODNESS AND OLDNESS

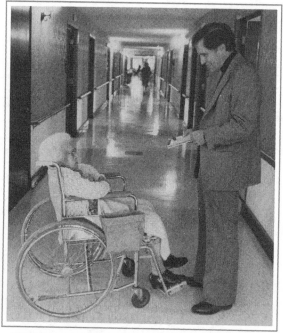

We live the hard questions of life until the end.

I didn't go to the Dunlap Care Center to preach the gospel. I went there to find it. I went there to touch the living past and in that energy to sense the momentum of God's grace. Mindful of that objective, I let the residents of the care center tell me of life, tell me of God. This is what they shared, directly and indirectly.

WHITE HAIR DOESN'T
MAKE A SAINT

Grandma has made her peace. Just look at her. She is the embodiment of one who is right with God and right with the world. Besides, she's lived her life. She's too old to think bad thoughts, too weak to cause trouble, and too isolated to be afflicted by the world's bad news. She has accepted death. She reads her devotional book every day, and she speaks with such innocence that you know she is at peace with everything. Well, at least she looks that way, and if she isn't . . . she ought to be.

There is an important value judgment in the last statement. Grandma is what we perceive and feel she ought to be. In fact, below the surface there are often very real struggles. There is sometimes a deep yearning for forgiveness, a cry against loneliness, the anger of being forgotten, the pondering of unresolved issues in the family, the fear of ever-increasing frailty and uselessness in boredom.

Certainly this is not every case. Nor, in the cases when it is true, is the issue always pushed to the extreme. Many people grow older with their lives in a relatively high state of contentment. Many people grow older with their lives bearing the cumulative witness of years of love and service to God. Many people indeed have become sensitive to what really matters in life and can see clearly in old age the world in which others are lost. Still, I have found that even such fortunate pilgrims have their struggles, their unfinished business.

Every point of transition in life is a time of new beginning with God—even if it is faced with the confidence of having lived well a lifetime of beginnings. In fact, the unfolding drama of old age bears a series of beginnings that takes as much courage to face as any challenge of earlier years. That goes even for those who in old age walk with a spiritually confident step.

At one meeting I shared an imagination exercise, directing the group to picture themselves standing in the crowd at Jericho as Jesus passed by. "Where do you see yourselves standing in that crowd?" I asked. The response caught me off guard.

"Somewhere back in the crowd, maybe behind three or four people," commented the angelic stereotyped "sweet little old lady" with a Bible in her lap. Her comment drew support from several others.

"Wait a minute," I said. "Why do you want to stand back in the crowd? Why don't you want to be up front where you can see him and call his name?"

"I guess," she replied with some embarrassment, "that I'm not sure how Jesus would respond as he saw me and saw through me. I think he'd be kind of disappointed." Again her response drew a consensus from others.

"I'm confused," I replied. "This is the same group that begins every hymn sing with 'In the Garden.' You know, 'And he walks with me and talks with me and tells me I am his own.'"

Everyone smiled with the irony as I had touched a nerve. Not everyone grows old totally confident of God's love, however they may appear. Sometimes the energy of the past that fills the present is a tad ambivalent. Sometimes it's more than a tad.

I'll call him Ernie. Ernie was a model of what every grandpa should be. Ernie meant kindness, quiet laughter, sensitivity, and thoughtful responses to the questions of the day. A picture of Ernie could be the cover of a greeting card; his could be the face of integrity that sells all-natural oatmeal cereal.

One Thursday I offered communion to my fellowship group. Certainly not all the participants were of my Christian persuasion. Thus, some chose not to participate. That was fine. Still, when Ernie declined I sensed it was more than a concern for denominational preference. Following the service, I went to Ernie's room to share with him my observation. "I'm not good enough to take communion," said Ernie. He continued in a whisper, "I've not led the best life." I tried to persuade him that it was for the Ernies of this world that the bread and wine were especially intended. He thanked me, stating once more that his life's history would not permit it. I asked if he wanted to talk about it. Ernie said no. I reached as far into Ernie's life as he would allow. So be it. I accepted Ernie, thankful for what he had shared, thankful that he at least let me sense what he brought to his private prayers.

I learned from Ernie. I learned something about the false images we have of white-haired innocence. I learned that not everyone who is ready to die is at peace with the world and, for some, that is the reason they are ready to die. I learned the meaning of a handshake and putting one's hand on the shoulder as sacramental gestures. I learned to pray for the healing of that which could not be expressed.

There were others who weren't at peace, especially those who spoke of unresolved family conflicts. Some of these conflicts had festered for over half a century. They were struggles not only of life but of God in life. In the end most struggles become that.

Again, not every person who grows old is less than content. Praise be to God that people often attain a certain sense of resolve, acceptance, and praise. However, that possibility must not blind those called to minister to older persons—as though all older persons live in spiritual Camelots with one foot in heaven. It isn't so. Acknowledging that it isn't so is a good start in realizing just how much we are really needed.

DOING AND BEING

We are born to serve. We hear that from the time we are first able to comprehend our relationship to God. We are the hands of God in the world. We are taught that life has its fulfillment, its meaning, in finding Christ in the face of the least of these thy brothers and sisters. What isn't mentioned is that if you live long enough, you become the least of these. It is a role for which lifelong "doing Christians" are not always well prepared.

A farmer supposedly has a lifespan of less than five years after retiring. In a sense, the farmer lives to work. When the work is over, a person's life sometimes loses its focus, its purpose, its joy, in spite of seemingly being a time when a person is free at last, free at last!

Retirement is not always what it's made out to be. Neither is Christian retirement. We are told that we are called to serve God until we die. In serving God we find God. God lives in us as God's love flows through us like the water of a river. What then does that say to an older person who no longer is able to be an obvious doer, one whose financial resources are gone, whose world has gone on by? What does it say to one who is becoming, though unwilling to acknowledge it, one of the least of these?

By the standards of our own earlier values, we come to a place of living in spiritual retirement. With that comes a judgment. If oneness with God is experienced in actively, sacrificially serving God, what happens when the serving slows down? When the river doesn't flow like it once did? The world honestly doesn't need us, and though God certainly is there, even God really isn't using us anymore. In candid moments one might hear, "Why am I still around? What good am I?" Sense within these questions one even more urgent, "Where is God in the living?" Aunt Clella's response, "At least I can still pray for others," spoke of her convictions. It also spoke of her awareness of how usefulness defines one's worth even in the eyes of God.

Perhaps you are ready to shout, "Wait a minute! People are of infinite worth even if they aren't 'useful' as the world understands that term. Besides, Aunt Clella *is right.* You can pray flat on your back, and prayer is a healing force, even as to move mountains. Yet even if her faculties should go and she couldn't form prayerful thoughts she would still be of value, and the spirit of God would be accessible to her even to the point that she bears all the more the face of Christ as she becomes even more 'the least of these.'"

Both perspectives have merit and warrant further thought. We *are* like a river, receiving and yielding fresh water. We do find oneness with God in being consumed by God's ongoing creation. That is, at least to an extent, and certainly to the end of life. That is, if life will let it happen. In most cultures, the old have a natural, obvious use in connecting the present to the past and by bestowing the value of their blessing. That such blessings for us are wasted away is everyone's loss. Furthermore, the waste is not just the loss of a person's story and its life-giving energy, but also that person's usefulness, that person's "work" in the community of faith.

To seek out the old and to do our duty once every three months—talking at them, amusing them, and filling them with our laughter and our words, without *needing* to listen, to probe, and to absorb for our own growth the lives of these people—is to deny in large measure the very spiritual gift of God one is trying to impart. The best way to fill these poor empty souls is to realize that they aren't poor, they aren't empty, and they certainly aren't worthless. They are indeed souls of worth. The best way to minister to their uselessness is to use them—use them, mindful that as we are open to them flowing into us, so are they experiencing their legitimate useful place in God's domain.

Such times of ministry may also demonstrate to the one who has come as a benevolent visitor, and whose life is a numbed rat race of coping, that just maybe he or she who came in a whirlwind to serve Christ was in fact the most impoverished of all.

The same basic concern challenges one of the basic assumptions of nursing homes themselves. It is a given that the nursing home is there to take care of the resident. The resident is occupied, kept active, entertained—all of which are passive for the resident. Seldom is it stressed that those residents who are capable are *openly expected* to care, actively to care, for each other—to pray for each other, to show concern for the hospitalized, to understand that they are in this together. Such an environment not only creates a home but also says to the resident, "You matter. You have a spiritual stake in each other's well-being. There are some things that *only you* can give each other."

The spiritual emphasis in most care facilities is a weekly roundup of "the usuals" with a rotating clergy person to speak. Such spiritual passivity is not enough. Perpetual spiritual fellowship is essential. That essential need should be vocalized as a central goal of staff, residents, and clergy.

Yes, doing is being, to an extent, but not entirely. In dying for Christ we live, yes, but there is more. *There is more.* Life is meant to be enjoyed. Beauty is truth. Wondering, delighting in life, is its own justification. Play is its own reason for being. It is not just a chance to catch our breath before we get back to healing, nourishing, and setting the world free in Christ's name. To those who are Type A doers, enjoying life for its own sake seems immoral, wasteful, and self-indulgent. They believe that if you must take a vacation, then do so as a means to an end; see it as a necessary relaxation so you can get back revitalized to God's work. Let the break inspire you so you can go back to the church with five new sermons to preach from all your leisurely readings.

No, no. Enjoying life is good because it is good. Sitting is good. It needs no justification other than that it produces joy, because joy is good. It is especially good if it is, from time to time, a shared joy.

Once, I was wrestling with a scripture and Christ came to me in a new way. Lost in wonder, I pursued it and pursued it until the demands of preaching stepped in. "What is the moral?" the little voice cried inside. "What is the lesson? The meaning? The bottom line?" There wasn't any, and trying to boil it down into a lesson destroyed it. I had come to see Christ in a different light. It made me wonder at God's love all the more. "Yes, but what? Wonder what?" I don't know, and I don't know that the question always matters. I just wondered, and the wondering was enough. I enjoyed the wondering without it being trivialized into usefulness.

I want more of that in my life. I want to grow old wondering well. I want to grow old in

the company of those who wonder in a praise
of silence, half sentences, and mysteries that
refuse to be made into three-point sermons.

In like manner, the worth of older people
is found in more than discovering the wealth
of their empowered past and their ability to
care for each other. Sometimes it was nice to
be together to wonder, to play, and to pray,
because *it was nice*. Sometimes we can
wonder better together than alone. In time, I
came to enjoy my group for no other reason
than that I enjoyed the people. Just being
there was enough reason to be there. God
was there too. God was in the being there,
delighting in the wonder. The wonder didn't
lead anywhere. It didn't cause anything to
happen but more wonder. That was enough.
That's what comes with time in communion.
As one gets older, there is more time to
wonder especially if it's good communion. The
wondering is good because it is good. God is
there. Life matters in the delight of it all.

Being and doing. They are in a dance. It is
a dance that is not intended to be resolved,
nor is it over when one's legs can't match the
music.

PART IV:
SACRED TRADITION

The living past throbbing into the present.

SACRED TRADITION

Tradition, traditional, traditionalism: These terms are usually taken to convey conservatism, sameness, holding on, and holding back. They suggest certainty, order, and caution. They may imply other notions: homespun, roots, nostalgia, rose-colored glasses, walking backward into the future.

Tradition—it means all that, doesn't it? Well, if it does, it could mean more. Tradition could mean more than the "good old days" lightly sprinkled like some holiday seasoning. It could mean more than bragging about one's heritage and the mandate to live up to our imaginings of our ancestral values.

Traditional living does not have to mean living in the past. Rather, it can mean claiming the living past that throbs into the present. It can mean discerning the rhythm of the pulse of all the yet living risks and adventures it took to get to this moment. Traditionalism can be the appreciation of all that it means to sing, "Safe thus far," mindful of just how unsafe it has been and how precarious the times are as we pick up the song and live and work by faith.

The question is: What is our tradition of tradition? How have we been conditioned to live with the past? Too often the picture of tradition is a place to hide, to escape from now. Consequently, some people do just that —they live their traditional lives hiding in the past—even as some dismiss tradition for the same reason. They are determined not to hide from anything, at any cost. Caught in the middle are the old, those who are treated patronizingly as living mementos of the good old days by some and avoided as irrelevant dinosaurs by others. They are the living face of tradition. Above all, they are the wasted blessing of tradition. In their living is the empowerment, the rippling energy, the continuity of hoping, the hoping of half of human history.

There is such a richness for those of us who dare to claim it, claim it because *we need it*. We need tradition in the most vital, sacred sense of the word. The church goes out of its way to see that ministerial candidates are prepared to speak well, to proclaim the good news. We should be equally concerned that they can listen well, discern the winds of the past, and savor the partial truths whispering of what is to be.

I believe that a part of any pastor's preparation should be to journey out into the wilderness of the home of a shut-in or a nursing home and find, in part, her or his consecration to carry hope to the next generation.

Perhaps in such listening a true ministry *to* older persons might begin. If it does, it will begin because it is born of what the older people bring to the pastor.

Again, ministry is an art. Ministry is at its best when pastors begin to tinker, to delight, and to play with what they find, *on the terms given by what they find*. Consequently, this little book does not end in an outline or with a how-to-do-it program. Instead, it challenges the reader to rethink the need for tradition in his or her life and to consider the essential role of tradition in discerning the sacred. This is a *call* to risk the adventure of touching the sacred energy of half of human history, absorbing it, being absorbed by it, and finding a part of your life's blessing in it.

If such possibilities excite you, then dare to enter into ministry, to share the blessing and to be blessed. Dare to begin with the most basic situations.

This venture into ministry could be as simple as claiming a new determination to make the most of your next visit with older family members. Talk with them about how their memories and mementos might become an important part of the next holiday gathering. No one has more to gain (or lose) in such sharing than our own families.

You might continue such a ministry by selecting the home of an older person in the neighborhood, especially a shut-in, and proceeding to knock regularly at that door. In these visits, look beyond your initial impressions of knickknacks and faded pictures. Be mindful that such items are the artifacts of a life and, thus, each item becomes a window of the experiences in which it was acquired.

As it becomes appropriate, seek the stories contained in albums and boxes of memorabilia. Touch the energy of those years with the feelings of your own struggles and joys. In your seeking be prayerfully mindful that God is revealing, creating, and blessing in that moment—blessing two people in the bond of generations as each gives meaning to the other.

As you develop your sensitivities to the needs and blessings of older persons, dare to carry this concern to a nursing home. Open its door determined to find its gifts. Talk with an administrator about your need to find meaning in such a facility and about your willingness to come regularly and to share in the lives of the residents. Perhaps such an interest might spark a group meeting as discussed earlier (see page 22).

Then again, perhaps the person reading this book is a nursing home administrator or director. If so, I challenge you to provide more than a passive, make-do ministry to your people. Dare to challenge the local churches —the laity and the clergy—to put aside outdated, misinformed, and condescending (though well-intended) views of nursing home residents. Talk with church people concerning their fears and awkwardness in coming to a nursing home. Discuss with clergypersons their true feelings about leading worship at the home. Wonder aloud with them what blessings are theirs to claim by coming to the home and listening, really listening, and finding the sacred in room after room of wasted tradition.

Dare to believe you have a facility that is a place of life with energy to give. The awareness and cultivation of that spiritual energy doesn't just happen. It exists when those in charge of nursing homes become determined to stop the image of the home as a place to be pitied and avoided. You are not a caretaker of hell on earth. If heaven's blessing is to be found under your roof, it will happen because you take the initiative to confront your community's stereotypes. That includes the churches. That includes the clergy.

Finally, be mindful that what took place in this book happened over a period of six years. To listen well is to wait well and to be sensitive to even the slightest gift that comes in the waiting.

God's grace is experienced in more than bold, broad, obvious strokes of the brush. Sometimes it's the fine strokes and the subtleties, which take time to discern, that bear the greatest meaning.

Perhaps in the end, the final gift of all is that in seeking the energy and meaning in older persons' lives, we will claim the courage to be sensitive to other abandoned corners of God's domain—those groups of people we have avoided, people in many kinds of prisons, people with diseases that frighten us, people still fighting wars that ended two decades ago. What greater gift could the old give us, what greater tradition could they establish, than to help those who are younger see more clearly a God who thrives amidst the forgotten?

EMPATHETIC KNOWING

It may be that the future belongs to those of multiple ways of knowing. One way of knowing is learning to listen well, and in the witness of this work, to listen well to our elders.

Empathetic knowing is more than an inherited gift of time and caring; it is an awareness of the depth and beauty of others, cultivated with much intentionality. Empathy is learned. Listening well is learned.

The lives discovered in this volume hopefully inspire the reader to see the blessing waiting to be given by the aged. Even more, it is hoped that empathy toward some becomes an inspiration of empathy to a hurting, frenzied, fearful world.

What greater gift could our elders avail than to help us discover a grammar of listening, a discipline of empathetic knowing, an enlightenment to a more humane, engaged and accepting openness to all people?

J.A.C.

ABOUT THE AUTHOR

Reverend James A. Campbell, D. Min. served for forty years as a pastor, with an emphasis on ministry with elders. The Iowa Health Care Association bestowed on Rev. Campbell "Iowa Clergy of the Year" for his model of creative listening in geriatric settings. The ministry with elders took new form and emphasis as Rev. Campbell was in mission work in Alaska and the Russian Far East. From this came a program of nurturing spiritual community and blessing of the aged that he developed with Alaska Native elders and called, "Giving Voice." Rev. Campbell is the author of seven books on ministry. He lives in retirement with wife, Maggie, in Beulah, Colorado, where he continues his interest in discerning different ways of knowing. He seeks to find how each way of knowing unfolds into wonder, and wonder into the sacred.

Made in the USA
Charleston, SC
10 May 2016